GW01315974

ABOUT THE AUTHOR

Orsetta Lopane was born in Rome in 1983 and achieved a Master's Degree in Languages and International Communication from Università degli Studi Roma Tre, Rome Italy.

In 2013 she completed a professional certificate course in Translation and Conference Interpretation at Gregorio VI University in Rome, Italy.

Professor of Cambridge International and English Literature, translator, simultaneous conference interpreter.

She has translated various books, the latest is "Senza via di Scampo" - Masaji Ishikawa for Newton Compton Editori.

Bilingual since she was born (English and Italian); she has always lived in international environments and studied in American schools with a background of international studies, she also speaks perfectly French and Spanish.

She has always travelled around the world spanning from Asia, the North Pole, Africa and to South America.

She is also the founder of the travel blog "The Chignon traveler", where she loves to write and give tips about her trips to new and amazing places.

The Last Waltz on Earth

Orsetta Lopane

"I know that I know nothing"

- SOCRATES

"Your freedom ends where mine begins"

- OLIVER WENDELL HOLMES, Jr.

To MABO my guardian angels.

To Andrea, my wave.

To Eleonora, a special friend.

The Last Waltz on Earth

ANIMALS AND THE 3.0 ERA

On the maps of the ancient Romans, on top of the African internal regions appeared this Latin phrase "hic sunt leones" which meant unknown land.

It would take years to describe this vast continent, which is not our task, but just to grasp at some important issues, in order to create our own opinions and ideas.

It is an immense country bursting with deserts, rivers, lakes, valleys. This is why only in the 17th century the Europeans left with their first expeditions.

When they discovered that it was also a very rich country in terms of natural resources (ex. coltan, petrol, iron, diamonds, natural gases and gold) things got worse.

But what is Coltan?

The mineral coltan is one of the resources that is playing an important role in the technological revolution. Coltan itself is a vessel for technology minerals, tantalum and niobium.

Coltan, or columbite tantalite, is an ore from which niobium and tantalum are extracted. These minerals are often found together, but have very different properties and applications; nearly 80 percent of the world's niobium is used in high-strength, low-alloy steels, while tantalum is key for the world's electronics industry.

The US Geological Survey lists Brazil, Canada and Australia as the leading producers of tantalum and niobium mineral concentrates.

The second largest miner is Rwanda, located next to the DRC in Central Africa. Rwanda was also involved in a bloody civil war, which resulted in violence and instability. There has been widespread speculation that much of Rwanda's mineral production comes from smuggling in resources from other countries.

The aftermath of war has left both nations vulnerable to militia, and other groups that often fight over control of the valuable mineral resource and mining sector. In the two nations, coltan is often mined through artisanal operations.

Coltan mining has also caused significant destruction of gorilla habitats in the DRC. As the UN Environment Program has reported, "The number of eastern lowland gorillas in eight DRC national parks has declined by 90 percent over the past 5 years, and only 3,000 now remain." Gorilla habitats have been reduced as forests are cleared to make way for mining operations.

In addition, the Jane Goodall Institute of Canada states that there have been reports of armed rebel groups and miners "eating meat from chimpanzees, gorillas, and elephants in the Kahuzi Biega National Park and on the Okapi Wildlife Reserve."

Mountain gorilla habitats have also been impacted by the illegal coltan mining and smuggling industry. The ongoing conflict and issues around mining and sourcing coltan have prompted calls to the Congolese government and local leaders to strengthen the conflict minerals law.

This is only an example of the "new aftermath" concerning Africa's exploitation.

Unfortunately, this international colonization policy has led to the problems that we encounter today: too many deaths, malnutrition, endemic diseases, civil wars, social unrest, exploitation of the land and of its people.

A recent and very sad phenomenon is named "land grabbing" which represents a threat to the developing countries.

Land grabbing – is a new form of economic Colonization. The protagonists are the developed countries which buy at a very low cost vast extensions of agricultural land in the Southern parts of the world to implant monocultures.

As human populations expand, more land is being converted to agriculture.

Consequently, elephant habitat is shrinking and becoming more and more fragmented, so that people and elephants are increasingly coming into contact and conflict with each other.

With human populations continuing to grow across their range, habitat loss and degradation and conflict with communities will remain major threats to elephants' survival.

The Anthropocene era, a name coined for us, is namely the current geological age, viewed as the period during which human activity has been the dominant influence on climate and the environment.

The aftermath is immense but in this vast country many natural environments are disappearing due to indiscriminate exploitation of the land and the resources of the wars and of poaching.

The illegal hunters won't renounce to the money gained by the trade of elephant tusks and rhinoceros horns which play an important role in the market of the extreme East.

In some cases, poaching animals to use their body parts for traditional medicine is the primary reason why an animal faces the risk of extinction.

The Chinese government has legalized the use of endangered tiger and rhino products for "medical" purposes, there is still a lucrative trade in the body parts in China, where thousands of captive tigers are bred for ineffective traditional cures.

Unfortunately, education and indoctrination are the only solutions. Ignorance is the waiting room of wickedness.

I have been travelling since I was born, seen so many countries, witnessed so many experiences that opened my mind, in a sort of odd way, I have become a different person, detached from the microcosm, the city I live in, the burden carried, is much heavier and most of the times, difficult to describe to whom hasn't seen the outside world.

These ears have heard such sad stories in Africa, in Asia, these eyes have cried looking at the elephants in the orphanages undressed by their jewels.

Despite a ban on the international trade in ivory, African elephants are still being poached in large numbers.

Tens of thousands of elephants are being killed every year for their ivory tusks.

The ivory is often carved into ornaments and jewelry; China is also here the biggest consumer market for such products.

5 A.M in the morning, this is what I'm thinking about while our jeep is running through one of the greatest parks in South Africa, the Kruger. Witness of this cold wind (it's winter) that caresses my face and hair, I know that today is no joke.

Our guide was born here and knowing we are pro travelers starts to tell us all about this park. Most of the stories are sad, all connected to what I have explained previously. Is it possible that every single corner of the Earth and every damn place I have been visiting has something shocking to teach me?

Why are humans so evil?

Only for this money God called Dollar, Euro, Yen, whatever!

So here we are, about to see the Big five, the most majestic and amazing animals in the whole entire world - Lion, Buffalo, Elephant, Leopard, Rhinoceros.

They double check our documents and finally let us in.

They told us that poachers try to get inside in any possible way…

It is not only the rate at which these animals are being killed, but the manner in which this happens that has many South Africans calling for more stringent action. In a recent incident in the Kruger National Park (KNP), poachers hacked the horn from a rhino while it was still alive, leaving the animal stumbling about with its face mangling to a bloody mess until the traumatized animal was spotted by horrified tourists.

Since January, the country has lost almost 100 rhinos, with the Kruger National Park (KNP) being the hardest hit in terms of numbers at 33, followed by the North West Province at 18, 12 from the Gauteng Province. The least affected province has been the Eastern Cape Province with a loss of only two rhinos. The provinces' protected areas lost 32 rhinos while the private sector lost 27 rhinos. Four black rhinos have also been poached.

The guide told me that poachers can also spend days in the park in order to accomplish their cruel homicides. They sleep on trees and hide themselves from the rangers until they find and kill their preys.

The sun was rising, Simba was waking up asking himself if this was his last day, our Jeep was rolling in as fast as possible.

The black trees were hiding from the pink and orange sun, in front of our small and naïve eyes.

The Hyenas looked tired after having spent their nights hunting, maybe this is the reason why they seemed candid. We started to see all of God's magnificent creatures, they were drinking by a lake, all together. Crocodiles and hippos, one next to the other, swimming and making all of their strange and funny noises - Zebras, giraffes...

Oh, good morning world!

Then there they were...

Twenty, thirty lions and lionesses all gathered together with their sweet and fragile cubs sitting on a colossal rock, monitoring the circle of life from up above.

The lionesses had an attentive look, they were always on guard, trying to protect their little ones.

Once, many years ago, they were the masters of the lands, born and raised there. Now they are locked in natural reserves living in continuous danger.

Then, in the distance, I saw the fairest animal in the world, a mammal that balances all of the laws in nature.

The elephant.

Elephants never abandon each other. If an elephant is injured, the other elephants try to assist him, even if it puts them in danger to stay and help. If an elephant has to move slowly because injured or aged, the other elephants too, in the group, will move slowly with him.

If an elephant dies, the whole group mourns the death.

They were beautiful, you know why?

Because they were still wearing their clothes, they weren't deprived of those jewels given by mother nature.

The tusks were shining bright as they were all walking towards us.

They wore them with such boldness, pride, dignity and grandeur. It was the first time, after many years, that I could admire again an elephant with its fangs on.

It felt like being in a Walt Disney cartoon, the elders in the front and the little, all happy, in the back, marching in perfect rows, slowly heading to the river.

It was time to go and take a bath!

"A-weema-weh,

a-weema-weh,

a-weema-weh,

a-weema-weh.

A-weema-weh

a-weema-weh,

a-weema-weh,

a-weema-weh.

In the jungle, the mighty jungle The lion sleeps tonight!"

BHUTAN'S TIGER SKIN

I give a fast look at the world map, pinpoints everywhere but the most dotted is Asia...

I realize that once a year, an airplane has always zoomed me there without realizing that I have visited most of the countries, I look closely, only one is missing... Bhutan!

Yes, a place that unfortunately, nowadays has become so instagrammable and fashionable, in fact the publishing house Lonely Planet has awarded the first prize 2020 for best travel to Bhutan.

Sometimes it's difficult to find a travel buddy, I have accomplished that my trips are off the normal traveler's beaten track (not for long though) ergo - during the years - since travelling has become so mainstream due to the social networks, every place is reachable, touchable, storyable aka instagrammable, I have detached from this dictat and created my way of exploring.

One decides to visit some countries during the low season, to explore unknown lands and parts that still haven't been raped, namely exploited.

We already know who the fault belongs to: we can call it globalization, turbo-capitalism, turbo-materialism, homologation, but first of all everything began with colonization…

Colonialism is a forced social change of every single country that has been mutilated of its identity.

It has become one globalized world, to my astonishment, to find an espresso in a place so far, hidden and impossible to reach wasn't so difficult.

The speediness of the transportation has pulverized the planetary distances. International connections are faster and economic, it's the effect of globalization, the process of economic social and cultural integration between the world's countries.

With a click of, the mouse, or with the touch of a finger on the screen, we can interact with anyone and buy anything. With internet, the online commerce has developed colossally, everything managed by the monsters of the ecommerce like Amazon and Ebay. Internet and the TV channels have transformed our planet in a "global village".

A small, landlocked country nestled deep in the Himalayas between India and China, Bhutan is characterized by steep mountains and deep valleys, which led to scattered population settlement patterns. The country is famous for its unique philosophy – Gross National Happiness (GNH) – which guides its development.

Almost completely cut off for centuries, it has tried to let in some aspects of the outside world while fiercely guarding its ancient traditions.

The Bhutanese name for Bhutan, Druk Yul, means "Land of the Thunder Dragon" and it only began to open up to outsiders in the 1970s.

The Wangchuck hereditary monarchy has wielded power since 1907. But Bhutan became a two-party parliamentary democracy after elections in March 2008.

Limited tourism, closely controlled by the government, began to develop in Bhutan in the mid-1970s. In the early 1990s, however, the tourism industry was privatized, and since that time the volume of tourists, tourist facilities, and tourist income increased monumentally. In the early 21st century there remained a government-imposed daily tourist tariff (250$ x day) to ensure significant tourist input into the economy.

One could say that the price is very high, but this sort of organization keeps all of the uninterested social travelers away and attracts the ones that are profoundly captured by this amazing land.

Bhutan is (in my mind) the perfect example of "how to cope" with global tourism in Asia.

Yet here we are on plane that will take us to Delhi (India for the 10th time) and then to Paro.

As soon as we landed, we noticed the difference between India and Bhutan, so close but so different, a breathing oxymoron. Me and my friend Alexandra were speechless. Everything was clean, only one who has travelled through these countries and mountains can understand our astonishment when I say, not a plastic bottle on the streets…

Our Sherpa was waiting for us, wearing his typical skirt, similar to the Scottish ones, but this was orange, yellow, green, red and pink.

Bhutan is the only place in the world that has Buddhism as its state religion - says the guide - and off we go for another of our adventures!

From there we started to visit all of the dzongs and stupas around the country like narcotics, met thousands of monks, what captured my attention was the difference one can touch from our Western world.

We felt like foreign particles.

For us, these were expeditions of discovery.

Yes, this land is still surviving without globalization, the law of opposites is still alive, not like India and Nepal that have bowed down to this great God called Dollar. This place, on which I'm stepping on now has remained crystal clear, this is what I'm thinking while we are walking at 3400 meters of altitude (no joke) with our Sherpa, and out of the blue he says:

"It's raining let's hope to meet no tigers!"

I asked skeptically: "Tigers?"

Sherpa: "Yes there are a lot of tigers around here."

Thankfully we reached the car without meeting one, and headed to the most overwhelming monastery that I had seen in my entire life, ab absurdo, better than the Taj Mahal or Chichén Itzá…

The Gangtey Monastery, generally known as Gangtey Goenpa or Gangtey Monastery, is an important monastery of Nyingmapa school of Buddhism, the main seat of the Pema Lingpa tradition. It is located in the Wangdue Phodrang District, in the western part of Bhutan.

Situated atop a hill at an altitude of 3400 m, Gangtey Monastery (also known as Gangtey Sanga Choeling Goemba) offers a stunning view of Phobjikha valley. This venerable monastery was founded in 1613 by Je Kuenga Gyaltshen.

Chronicle: 26 of July 2019, low, low, low season, raining heavily the whole day, loads of kilometers to get there, we get out of the car, wrap ourselves around two rain jackets, start walking in this little village made of 10 houses, at 3400 meters of altitude.

I can still hear the same sound I heard a couple of months ago, OOOOMMMM. The monks were meditating and from all of the windows you could hear that strong sound calling, OM... Sherpa told us that there are two types of monks: the ones that have no money (namely obliged to enter the monastery) and the ones that feel the calling...

We gazed at many that had received this gift, delighted to live there, to pray the whole day and to study, some were playing with the cats but others were reading.

Buddhists believe in reincarnations and here in Bhutan it is thought that one has two spirits, one sitting on a shoulder and one on another, they are the ones that will define and judge your actions throughout all your entire life.

We started walking and taking some pictures (always with respect) and we noticed that half the monastery had been destroyed by the earthquake, but there were little kids living inside these tiny houses.

Inside Gantey, all of the walls were colored and the paintings were mind-blowing, there was no light because the thunderstorm of the day before had blustered away the electricity, but to our astonishment we saw 30 little monks sitting in the dark listening to their Guru. He was explaining the parable about the good and evil.

He was the only one that had power, using the torch to read and to explain.

After many weeks of twist and turns, my small heart did not beat noiseless that day, it was literally exploding inside my chest.

We were there, up above the clouds, with monks all dressed in orange and red singing and praying; I had accomplished one of my dreams, getting there, not an easy thing to achieve for a common traveler.

The day was dying, Sherpa said we had to leave, the road we had to traverse now was highly dangerous due to the continuous landslides that the day before on that street had killed two people. Rain was pouring down, soaking wet, Alexandra who had travelled more than me, was smiling, I guess she was thinking more or less the same things I was.

And out of the blue this flash back rolls in:

– She thought about the first time she met that girl.

She was sitting on a wall all dressed in blue.

A dichotomy in that huge American School.

It was her first day in that new microcosm and Alexandra immediately went to greet her.

From that moment the fil rouge grew thicker and thicker.

Alexandra was special, she was always nice to people and brilliant with her friends.

That little girl was forced to grow up very early, and while it was happening also the hurricane inside her soul was evolving.

Every little thing she did was magic, it seemed as though she sowed every problem with a silver string.

If something got broken, she would fix it with that golden glowing glue similar to the one used by the Japanese.

She remembered the day, where she cleaned that boat full of blood, without saying a word, helping her...

And now it was such an emotion to travel with her and share some pieces of life together, a puzzle which had started 26 years ago. –

With sadness we start walking backwards out of the monastery, we didn't want to miss a thing, in fact there he comes, passes in front of us, the most beautiful monk of all, strolling under the rain wearing a pair of black crocs, a red kesa and a chupa chups in his mouth, the perfect blend of globalization my eyes will ever see and witness in their entire life.

On the extreme peak of that mountain, he was the real traveler, except his journey was inward...

© Encyclopædia Britannica, Inc.

IN NEPAL

That was my second chance, I went there 20 years ago,

when everything was unspoiled and untouched

when the big earthquake still didn't show up.

My friend and I desired to go back and admire that jumbo mountain named the Everest.

One of the highest, they say.

Chronicle: Here we are, just landed in Kathmandu.

Pollution, dirt, incivility people and dogs dying on the streets, skeletons walking, this is the scenario,

nitty gritty reality.

The city seems to have no suburbs, which normally prepares one gradually with the encounter of downtown, here everything emerges out of the dark.

Your eyes see and your heart aches and screams at the sole sight in front of this horror.

We head to Pashupatinath, today, they're going to celebrate the great God Mahadeva - adolescents orange fully dressed - infinite rows, only to get in the sacred temple and to swim in the merciful and miraculous river.

People converging on the river, singly and in groups, columns of pilgrims. The lame on crutches. Aged virtual skeletons, some carried on the backs of the young, others exhausted, twisted, crawling with great difficulty on their own along the asphalt. We joined this mystery play too.

But today many have come to mourn their dearest ones,

I don't want to know what you feel when you see your beloved burn.

Cremated, incinerated on wood and straw.

Pashupatinath, is an incredibly holy place.

Thousands of faithful are already there, pushing their way who knows where and why, others sit in the lotus position, stretching their arms up towards the nirvana.

A river runs straight the heart of the temple complex and it metamorphs into India, connecting to the Holy Ganges River.

When someone in Kathmandu dies, the body is purified, cleaned and prepared at Pashupatinath.

It is then wrapped in cloth and placed on a stone block next to the river. Pieces of wood are stacked under, around and on the body.

Straw is also spread over the body before it is lit on fire.

The face and feet of the body are left exposed the entire time.

After 3-4 hours of burning the cremation is complete and the ashes and remains are swept into the river.

This process is part of the Hindu belief that they will be reincarnated.

Dozens of burning pyres…

I felt so tiny.

On the other side of the river bank I prayed for that desperate wife that was kissing her husband for the last time.

Words can't describe the whirlwind of feelings that have permeated in my heart.

It's cathartic.

There, you feel alive, you suddenly realize you are living, smelling, inhaling, tasting that very, small, slight, itsy bitsy moment.

Yet then…

The stunning beauty, coiled up in the caves, we saw them, the great Sadhus.

Many asked for money in order to take a picture of them, but how could they live otherwise?

This has become one of their jobs, also the Gurus have bowed down to the great God of money.

Meanwhile one of them was baptizing me:

"Happiness, good and long life!" Said the old sage as he was gracefully putting some red powder on my forehead and tying thrice on my wrist a little golden ribbon.

Next, we headed up the hill out of the crowds into the empty forest to unleash what we had just witnessed.

Only monkeys and birds made a noise.

We slowly made our way through the winding forest trail passing countless graves, overgrown by weeds.

Yesterday, the heart was beating fast, blood was rushing through my veins, Sherpas say they are the last Masters left,

and we have seen them…

In these places you feel like being in the underworld,

a perpendicular disharmony if you look at their golden colored saris.

You feel like the gray dust you have seen for days, you float atop the waves for a while but very soon you sink and vanish...

After having traveled in these countries my dear friends, I need to think, my soul and my eyes need to decant and digest what they have seen because it'll be hard to find magic places as cathartic and absorbing like Nepal.

MOTHER TERESA

Here we are, again, on a different track.

Immobile I have planned and fantasized to go volunteering.

One of my greatest dreams has always been to fly and see Mother Teresa's little helpers.

So freedom kidnaps me one more time for another life's ticket to ride.

Her orphanages are spread all-over Asia, especially in India and in Sri Lanka.

I had already been in India to visit them and to donate the money I had.

But these letters and words that stuck,

tied,

sown,

one to the other will spring a feeling inside you

are totally consecrated for my trip in Sri Lanka.

Colombo,

your eyes start to grasp, they can't handle all of that blazing mess,

those colors, the smell of the incense dancing out ubiquitously along with cows, cats, dogs, people and children begging for money, the social fabric of all the religions buried and stitched in that city.

Gazillions of yellow tuk tuks are hurtling in front of me, mules carrying carts, humans still whip and exploit the animals in a cruel way.

I have seen their dead bodies lying on the floor.

We decide to rush before Mother Teresa closes her doors.

After a couple of hours, we finally arrive, it hasn't been easy to find this place without a map.

My heart's beating fast and blood's flying through my veins.

I have a look at the old, ugly black rusty gate and think:

"This is where the poor abandon their newborns."

We get in, a big and fat figure comes to receive us, but it's not the greeting I had expected.

No kindness, she seemed marble sculpted.

Later I understood, after you'll comprehend

Wait…

Don't judge.

I commence to talk to the sister and she introduces me to all of the others.

The first part was the most shocking, no the second, the first, oh both!

In front of my eyes all little cradles,

cribs full of orphans crying.

They were alive from a couple of weeks, already suffering, from the day they were born.

I think to myself, what kind of life could they have?

How much will they have to fight?

What color are their feelings going to be?

Black

Grey...

...and blue.

The sisters were all feeding them, making sure they were protected by the mosquito nets.

Why?

Because in many places in Asia and Africa, people and especially kids, still die if they are bitten by a mosquito.

They can contract malaria, dengue fever, since they are not vaccinated and die easily.

The money that I donated was used to buy the mosquito nets for the kids. One useful thing done in my life…

Then it happens that the sister brings you upstairs, in the first room there were the youngsters affected by the Down's syndrome, we couldn't get in, only they could.

In the second big room I see around 20 kids dancing and singing, so I fearlessly take my shoes off and get inside.

Two little girls come and take my hand, carrying me in the middle of the room and start laughing.

These two little slips start climbing on my legs like cubs, reaching for my chest, I found myself having four little mademoiselles willing to kiss and embrace me.

For a second, they reminded me of when I was in Rome at the dog shelter and in the morning I found abandoned puppies in front of the gate.

The despair was the same, their need of love resembled those pups.

It seemed as though for a second they wanted to stick their heart to mine.

I'll never forget that time of my life, they didn't even know who the hell I was, poor little creatures begging for love.

A vortex of emotions was immediately tattooed inside my skin forever, when I'll be old, I'll still remember those faces and smiles.

Little kids asking for a bit of attention, from me, a stranger to their fragile grey lives.

A traveller like me, a ghost, a specter that had flown from the other part of the world to see them, to donate a morsel of help.

After having spent a couple of hours playing, the nun calls and says: "You don't have to touch the kids, you mustn't hug them! We never do it, so you know, they suffer less, the moment they go…"

"Oh, yes I understand, I'm sorry sister"

Today, their eyes have talked to me, they have begged for love, but I couldn't give it to them, I'll never be able to."

I was shocked, empty-handed, feeling incapable of doing anything, at a loss even to know where to begin.

I cried when we left, powerless, helpless, stupid human.

TAIL UP!

Mirissa is a small town in the Southern coast of Sri Lanka, located in the Matara District of the Southern Province.

It is approximately 150 kilometers south of Colombo, the capital city.

I've been there only for one reason, to try to go and see one of the biggest animals in the world, the blue whale.

I have studied that these creatures migrate from Antarctica's cold water, from October to April and reach the warm tropical waters.

Do you know how many hazards they need to face to reach a destination?

One of the worst is whaling, ergo the hunting of whales for food and oil...

Whales may be taken and their meat and products commercially sold.

Entanglement in fishing gear is the leading threat for whales and dolphins around the globe, estimated to cause at least 300,000 deaths per year.

Whales and dolphins rely on critical habitats areas where they feed, mate, give birth, nurse young, socialize or migrate for their survival. In countless areas around the globe, critical habitats are under threat from a variety of human activities; including intense fishing, increased shipping, off-shore exploration of oil and gas and marine-based tourism.

Additional pressures include coastal construction, climate change, and pollution from a variety of sources. Only a tiny fraction of critical whale and dolphin habitats is protected from these threats, and greater protection is urgently required to prevent vulnerable populations from decline.

But hold on a sec, what about plastic?!

Plastic pollution causes great harm to the organisms, big and small. From tiny corals to majestic whales, more than 700 marine species are known to be killed either by the ingestion of plastic or entanglement - resulting in more than 100 million animal deaths a year, that we know of.

Right now there are more than 51 trillion pieces of plastic in the ocean. That's 51 trillion deadly hazards that animals need to avoid.

Made to be used just once, plastic can last forever in the environment. Once a plastic bag, abandoned fishing net or bottle cap have killed by entanglement, strangulation, suffocation or starvation, it simply has to wait for its victim to decompose to be released back into the environment. Plastic does not decompose; it will be ready to kill again soon.

What is the death toll?

Sea turtles: All seven species of endangered sea turtle ingest or are entangled by plastic. More than 50% of sea turtles eat plastic.

54% of all whales, dolphins and seals are impacted by plastic.

A 2019 study of dolphins, whales and seals in waters of the UK found that 100% of dead animals on their coast had ingested plastic.

In March 2019, a whale was found vomiting blood in the waters of the Philippines, dying shortly afterwards. Upon autopsy, it was found that almost 40kg of rice sacks, chip packets and balls of fishing gear had built-up in its stomach, causing a build-up of stomach acid which dissolved the walls of the whale's stomach and caused it to bleed internally to death.

Why do animals eat plastic?

Unlike humans, wild animals do not have the ability to discern plastic from "digestible" materials. Simply put, if it looks like food, or smells like food, or tastes like food or behaves like food, then it must be food.

Filter-feeding animals, like whale sharks and baleen whales, can ingest plastic by accident.

Plastic can release chemicals that smell like food, triggering species such as anchovies to find it.

Jellyfish-eating species, such as ocean sunfish and sea turtles, mistake plastic bags and balloon ribbons for jelly medusae.

Grazing and scavenging animals, such as cows, seagulls, dogs and camels, regularly eat plastic that has been contaminated with human food.

Plastic microbeads resemble fish eggs and are often eaten by jellyfish, egg-eating fish and filter feeders.

Seabirds that skim the ocean surface while flying, such as albatrosses, cannot differentiate floating food from litter.

Sonar of some animals can confuse plastic for squid and jellyfish.

Hunting seabirds mistake small pieces of suspended plastic, such as cigarette lighters, for small prey fish.

Red, pink and brown pieces of plastic debris are mistaken for shrimp.

How does it kill?

There is no quick death when it comes to plastic:

Jagged plastic can get stuck in their throats, causing them to suffocate or prevent them from regurgitating to feed their chicks.

Plastic can accumulate in animals' stomachs, making them feel full, stopping them from eating and resulting in starvation.

These mammals namely face so many calamities that you can only admire them once you study what they have to encounter.

It was an early morning when we got a little boat in a tiny harbor inside Mirissa, and forgot for one day about our ordinary life.

The sun was just rising on the Indian Ocean and we were about to cut through those waves, silently looking for those majestic creatures.

The Captain was one of those kind of men, who was born to linger his entire life at sea. He was Australian and had decided to spend his existence submerged by that entangling nature.

The sea that day was rough, and believe me when I tell you that the Ocean's waves are utterly different from the ones of the sea…

So I asked:

"Captain how many knots is the sea today?"

He replied:

"Well today's for pros, 9 meters! We're gonna have lots of fun!"

Oh, the waves of the Ocean are so infinite and black.

On that little boat, I happened to have all kinds of thoughts, while we started to sail away from the harbor and were contoured only by the big black ocean I saw some fins. Cap told me it was normal. They were sharks...

Then in the stillness of that grey rainy, windy day, with total devotion we started to wait.

With respect, we attended, minutes, became hours; then out of the blue we saw a spurt in the sea, purring...

They were coming!

I remember those moments as a pervading thrill.

I saw their heads. Then the beauty in their dance when they cracked those waves like transparent Sufis, praying to the Almighty and in extreme grace, they overwhelmingly showed their "tail ups!"

Finally, in the middle of that immense ocean, my dream came true...

We were so little in front of the majesty of Nature.

Big but fragile creatures, seemingly little babies.

It's hard to be an animal in a world dominated only by mean men.

How evil and wicked can you be to kill with such cruelty mothers and cubs on their way back home?

How would you feel if your loved ones were tortured and assassinated on their way home?

This is the holocaust of our animals not less important than the human's one.

This is the world we have created and live in.

You, can do something, live a life in which you can recognize yourself within.

AHIMSA'S TWIST AND TURNS

Close my eyes, use Wordsworth's powerful recollection in tranquility and everything's crystal clear.

I'm thrown there, once more, in a vortex of dizzying endlessness.

The smells, incense all around, mixed with the stench of the roads full of rubbish, plastic, cows and sheep eating garbage next to the old cars and tuk tuks passing and honking continuously their horns like crazy!

Old Delhi! Narrow, dusty, hot streets with their smell of tropical fermentation.

Crowds of people appearing and disappearing, dark faces.

Children making no sound, begging for money, food, attention.

A beggar shows me how the skin of his stomach is plastered to his spinal cord.

Gazillions of people walking, soaked skeletons, ad infinitum, pollution everywhere, welcome to India!

The twelfth largest world economy and the second for the most rapid growth after China.

It belongs to the group of the Brics (Brazil, Russia, China and South Africa).

BRICS is the acronym coined for an association of five major emerging national economies: Brazil, Russia, India, China, and South Africa.

Originally the first four were grouped as "BRIC" (or "the BRICs"), before the induction of South Africa in 2010. The BRICS members are known for their significant influence on regional affairs; all are members of G20.

India is also the third country in the world for what concerns the difference between rich and poor. Two thirds of the farmers, that live in small villages usually without electricity and drinkable water, own less than a hectare of land, or they labor the lands of the rich owners without mechanical tools, limited to sheer survival. The rich owners still treat them like slaves in 2020 A.D.

This country belongs to the British Commonwealth and it is the most populated country after China.

This immense country is still bound to the caste system. India's caste system, which splits up Hindus into different societal groups according to their work and birth, is thought by researchers to go back some 3,000 years.

In the system, Hindus are divided up into four classes based on the principle of "varna" which literally means "color": The Brahmins (the priestly class); the Kshatriyas (the ruling, administrative and warrior class); the Vaishyas (the class of artisans, tradesmen, farmers and merchants); and the Shudras (manual workers).

There are also people who fall outside the system, including tribal people and the Dalits, previously known as "untouchables," although the term is somewhat contentious.

The concept of "jati" meaning "birth," also underlies the caste system and causes its differentiation into thousands of sub-groups based on lineage or kinship that are difficult to define.

The system has led to the upper castes being privileged over the lower castes, which were often repressed by those higher up on the caste scale. For centuries, inter-caste marriage was forbidden, and in villages, castes mostly lived separately and did not share amenities such as wells.

The caste system was bolstered under the British Raj, which appointed only upper-caste Hindus to senior positions and administrative jobs. During the 1920s, however, protests led to the colonial administration introducing a system of quotas under which a certain percentage of government jobs were reserved for lower-caste Hindus.

After India attained independence in 1947, the country introduced laws to make discrimination against lower castes illegal and to improve their socioeconomic positions. Quotas were introduced for college admissions and jobs.

As a result, some Dalits have made it to leading positions, such as BR Ambedkar, who wrote the Indian constitution, and KR Narayanan, who was elected president in 1997.

Inequalities under the system still exist in modern India despite these measures, which have even served to reinforce the divisions to some extent. Violence based on caste has also erupted in recent times, much of it involving attacks on Dalits.

The caste system has also spilled over into other religions in India, with Christians, Muslims, Sikhs and Jains all employing similar forms of social stratification.

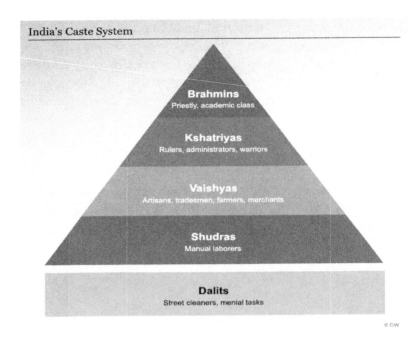

Hinduism is one of the world's oldest religions. It originated in India and is comprised of religious, cultural and philosophical concepts.

The Hindu concept of God is manifold. Hindus believe that there is one primary, omniscient and omnipotent deity called Brahma, but there are hundreds of thousands of deities that represent certain facets of the all-knowing, absolute and primary *Brahman*.

Hinduism is expressed and practiced in many different ways. The basic concepts include belief in reincarnation (*samsara*); right action (*karma*), duties, ethics or right ways of living (*dharma*); and liberation from the reincarnation cycle by living righteously (*moksha*).

The position of human beings in the world is not by chance, but in the behavior they held in their previous life.

Hinduism is responsible for the development of yoga and Ayurveda. Many Hindu practitioners also practice yoga.

Full of rituals and various observations, Hinduism is thought to be the oldest religion in the world, still practiced today. There is no specific founder or governing system; however, the governing texts or scriptures include the *Vedas*, the *Upanishads*, and the Bhagavad Gita.

Hinduism has many diverse rituals, including various festivals, *puja* ("worship") practices and pilgrimages. Hindus hold strong beliefs about non-violence, integrity, celibacy outside of marriage, cleanliness, purity, prayer, meditation and perseverance.

In Hinduism, yoga is a form of puja, a means of meditating to connect with the Divine and a way to develop the multi-faceted self (mind body and spirit).

People who adore India know exactly that the reason why it is so loved, is unknown.

She's dirty, poor, infect, polluted: sometimes, a liar a thief, corrupted, and damn indifferent.

Yet, once you meet her you just can't stay away from her.

In India you feel totally part of the Almighty's creation.

You never feel separated, aside, this is its allure.

Each single, tiny existence, mine and the one of a flower, is part of everything of a chain, thousands of shapes and forms called life!

In India you witness other emotions, you feel different and you think other thoughts. Maybe because time has never been contemplated as a straight line but as circular, past, present and future, which assumes a different meaning; here, the progress is not the main goal of the human actions.

Inside this country everything is contradictory, cruel. Yet life in this land, is also death, there is not pleasure without pain, no happiness without suffering.

In no other part of the world the juxtaposition of the opposites, beauty and heinous, richness and poverty is so dramatic, so bright as in India.

This is the magic duality that grabs every tourist and works as a spiritual catalyzer in order to discover the deed meaning and secret here.

One of the things that I love the most, is that the idea that men are not superior to animals and do not have the right to exploit them.

We are part of nature, nothing belongs to us, plus we are part of this chain, not out of it as main protagonists, our existence depends on nature.

Instead, the western civilization continues to cut down forests, pollute rivers, dry the lakes, depopulate the oceans, breed and slaughter each type of animal because the economy says that this produces wealth.

Oh, let me guess some still believe that the telly advertisements concerning how meat is good for your health is true!

Unfortunately, with this imprinting and mindset we have the mirage that more wealth means more happiness, so we use all our energies in consuming, thinking that life is an eternal Lucullian Roman banquet where you eat and vomit in order to eat once again.

The pity is that it has become so natural to us, plus we feel so separated from the others, the fil-rouge has been trenchantly cut.

This was the India that I first saw in 1993 when I was only a kid,10 years old and all of my relatives told my mom it would have been unwise bringing me there: "Poor girl, in that country!"

Nope, she was no crazy, she was a simple pioneer, my guru, she set the bar so high for me since I was born, this has been my luck throughout all of my existence, her philosophies…

But after some years I decide to go back and I will always return there throughout my entire life, what I encounter this very moment has totally shifted.

In only a decade this place is bizarre!

This "new India" is urban, rich, and pursues the "American dream" the naivety of western modernity and that now suffers of the same soul illnesses of the west.

This new country is the one that has been colonized and wounded from the scornful British dominance and that is once again attracted by a path which does not belong to them the great imperial one, ergo the U.S.

It's the one that has abandoned vegetarianism, that drinks alcohol, that has forgotten saris and wears blue jeans, that has cut its deep roots, that has rejected the great Mahatma and its ahimsa.

I'm talking about the emerging bourgeoisie living in Delhi, Bombay and Calcutta, that has turned away to millions of villages where the majority which has not been colonized lives nowadays.

It's the one that has wanted the atomic bomb, a natural right of course, but at the same time the abdication of a traditional strength not founded on weapons.

When I went back there, there were advertisements all over the place with written: "I'm back. Coca Cola!" The Ghandian ideology was dead and had left space to the big market of globalization. Along with Coke, came KFC, Mc Donald's, cable tv, American films and fictions, mobile phones, computers and so on.

At the same time, it has commercialized in small packages its traditions with books and manipulates of all of its teachings -like yoga for example- to the western world.

Travelling. The pleasure of a lifetime. The desire to bring my skin and my eyes to see the world since I was born.

A way of being, a job. Always the same, but always different: preparing to leave, go and then write about it.

Yet which was the sense in all of this? Why was it so stigmatized in my imprinting? I've never asked myself about it. Now, while I was watching those cremations in Benares that sense became crystal clear. If I'd never travelled I'd have nothing to talk about, think, say, feel, cry…

Travelling for me has always been a sort of spiritual growth, as if moving my body contributed to elevate the soul. The first time I have been India a master told me that sadhus, the homeless saints, must be like water, in continuous evolvement, or else they become stagnant…

India is the greatest lesson of humility one can receive in its entire life…

IN NORDKAPP

Four long years had passed, but that déjà vu brought her back to that trip with her husband, who would have ever known that it would have been her last?

The music was so loud they couldn't hear their voices in that hybrid car that was rolling like a flame on those majestic enormous roads, Stella was driving, but literally racing like crazy!

The Beatles, were on their Ipods 24/7 during that period of their lives, and Paul McCartney was shouting: "Get back, get back to where you once belonged!"

Oh, yes, that was life!

Rollin' on those fjords Stella and Gabriel, together for the rest of their lives, well they were just married from a couple of months, but she still wasn't aware of what was about to happen after that trip…

They had landed in Oslo, that capital seemed so modern, clean, civil, right.

It was August, and the sun during those months decides to never set on those countries in the far North of Europe.

Usually the citizens of the Scandic regions have to go through six months of day and six of night.

We can't imagine how difficult it must be, this is why it's one of the countries with the highest rate of suicides every year.

Norway is also called "the country of the fjords", which in fact are the most characteristic feature of its landscape.

A fjord is formed when a glacier retreats, after carving its typical U-shaped valley, and the sea fills the resulting valley floor.

Oslo during the summer was amazing, people singing in the streets, flowers, music, shops, people smiling and showing their excellent quality of life, driving their electronic Teslas through the blue city. They spent a few days admiring the monuments around and the museums, then headed and drove up to Nordkapp.

More or less 10.000 kilometers.

That trip was still stigmatized in her heart, those were the most beautiful roads Stella had ever seen, the first reindeers are so funny, when you discover they pass mostly their entire day peacefully on the road, cars pass by but they respect those animals.

Kilometers filled of green trees, reindeers and birds... Then the feeling of getting there, in the most northern part of the earth is something beyond words.

If she closes her eyes, she can still feel that thrill, driving as quickly as possible to get there before the gate closes, running between the ocean and his scent, so strong, with the seagulls shouting, she had always ran in her life, who knows why...?

Finally, they get there, the indication Nordkapp, imagine a place far northward, where the Atlantic Ocean meets the Arctic Ocean and their frigid waters mix.

That place is the North Cape, in Western Finnmark, Northern Norway. Here, the only dry land between you and the North Pole is the Svalbard archipelago.

This is a pinpoint on every traveler's path, you feel as though you've accomplished a little something, as if you've seen a part of the world.

She felt that cold breeze biting her cheeks, and that man next to her, so scared, insecure, dangerous but sacred, he seemed a white invisible shadow.

She felt so lone, why? Where was he? He was at war with his demons.

But how come she didn't notice that sickness deep inside his heart?

She still couldn't forgive herself for having committed such a big mistake...

After their marriage, he had raised up an iron curtain impossible to overcome.

It was as though she was still standing on the verge of North Cape's precipice, when Gabriel in the grip of his drunkenness tried to strangle her.

How could it be that those huge, big, beautiful hands could play the piano in such a delightful way and at the same time capable of killing her?

What happened to the love he promised to give her for the rest of their life?

He had played a role and now he was gently peeling his skin off by showing his real character and personality.

Her husband, a monster in her apartment.

That home where she was born and lived peacefully all her life with her parents, now he was trying to hurt her with his bare hands, while the earth was trembling under her feet, on that cold December night she had her epiphany, her moment of being...

She understood, Gabriel would have never changed, all of the stories she had heard on the news about women killed by their lovers.

Now she was there, maybe, it was her turn.

As usual, it happened again and again, so the right choice was...

She bowed down, recollected all the courage she found on the floor, ran to her dad, and showed him her bloody heart, torn apart, beating like crazy in her hot flaming hands.

Unfortunately, in that war he seemed to be the only one to line up on her side, friends said she had to try again...

Maybe, it happens, that due to these "friends" some innocent girls are ferociously killed...

That little woman, of 33, had many flaws but she was different for one thing, she had had a lot of courage since she was born and decided to follow the saddest path of all...

"Get back,

Get back,

Get back to where you once belonged…

Get back Jo Jo!"

NATURE'S LAST WALTZER

AN ADIEU TO NATURE:

"EVERY MINUTE A FOREST THE SIZE OF 20 FOOTBALL FIELDS IS CUT DOWN."

Nowadays, when we listen to the news or open our social networks we realize that we are constantly bombarded with words like: Climate change, melting of the ice caps, deforestation, loss of biodiversity, rising of the sea level and so on.

But do youngsters really understand what's happening?

I always try to bring some clear examples to the ones that are going to hold this world in their hands for some decades and then will pass on the baton to their sons.

They are nature's last chance.

According to recent studies things have drastically changed and every minute the situation is getting worse, right now as I am writing this chapter the BBC is talking about the fires that are going on in Australia since September 2019 and that now have reached the point of no return.

How many people die due to pollution problems?

How many animals have died in bushfires?

To my astonishment, a couple of weeks ago, some students told me that they don't care if animals die, or if the ice will melt, as long as their family will be fine they will not worry, if we all use this kind of mindset we have no hope at all.

Well, sometimes it feels really sad to listen to these comments, but I am sure that not all of our youngsters share this point of view!

"THE THINNING, changing and elimination of forests – deforestation; is not a recent phenomenon it is as old as the human occupation of the earth and one of the key processes of the history and our transformation of its surface:"

Michael Williams – Deforesting the Earth

As the world seeks to slow the pace of climate change, preserve wildlife, and support billions of people, trees inevitably hold a major part of the answer. Yet the mass destruction of trees deforestation continues, sacrificing the long-term benefits of standing trees for short-term gain.

Forests still cover about 30 percent of the world's land area, but they are disappearing at an alarming rate. Between 1990 and 2016, the world lost 502,000 square miles (1.3 million square kilometers) of forest, according to the World Bank an area larger than South Africa! Since humans started cutting down forests, 46 percent of trees have been felled, according to a 2015 study in the journal Nature. About 17 percent of the Amazonian rainforest has been destroyed over the past 50 years, and losses recently have been on the rise.

We need trees for a variety of reasons, not least of which is that they absorb not only the carbon dioxide that we exhale, but also the heat-trapping greenhouse gases that human activities emit. As those gases enter the atmosphere, global warming increases, a trend, scientists now prefer to call climate change. Tropical tree cover alone, can provide 23 percent of the climate mitigation needed over the next decade to meet goals set in the Paris Agreement in 2015, according to one estimate.

Farming, grazing of livestock, mining, and drilling combined account for more than half of all deforestation. Forestry practices, wildfires and, in small part, urbanization account for the rest. In Malaysia and Indonesia, forests are cut down to make way for producing palm oil, which can be found in everything from shampoo to biscuits to saltines. This production kills the forests and like a "fil rouge" the habitat of all of the animals like the orangutan.

In the Amazon, cattle ranching and farms particularly soy plantations are key culprits.

Here in the Amazon, lands are used mainly for raising cattle and the companies belong to American multinationals which namely need to trigger colossal quantities of meat in order to meet the need of the infinite and immense demand of the meat eaters and fast foods.

We could literally say that trees are forged into meat.

Instead in the forests of the Philippines, great Japanese industries cut down trees to obtain cardboard, which is essential for the packaging of objects that have to be sent around the world.

In the African forests like in Congo, Cameroon and Gabon wood is used to build the furniture that will be directed in big European shops.

Logging operations, which provide the world's wood and paper products, also fell countless trees each year. Loggers, some of them acting illegally, also build roads to access more and more remote forests which leads to further deforestation. Forests are also cut as a result of growing urban sprawl as land is developed for homes.

Not all deforestation is intentional. Some is caused by a combination of human and natural factors like wildfires and overgrazing, which may prevent the growth of young trees.

All of these shocks modify our local climate and the winds causing huge cataclysms, it also triggers the extinction of many animal species vital for the natural chai. We are all interconnected...

Deforestation is one of the main causes of climate change the polar ice has significantly reduced and so has the artic polar ice cap. This phenomenon unfolds various problems, in first place the habitat of the Artic is in extreme danger, animal species are in peril, for example the white polar bear is nearly extinct.

Why?

Simple, he has no land to walk on, the ice has melted and he's trapped to swim much longer distances.

In second place, this melting creates the rising of sea levels. Many regions will be submerged some are witnessing this problem right now. Take Jakarta for example or Venice…Just to name a couple…

So where will all of the people living in these cities go?

Deforestation affects the people and animals where trees are cut, as well as the wider world. Some 250 million people living in forest and savannah areas depend on them for subsistence and income, many of them among the world's rural poor.

Eighty percent of Earth's land animals and plants live in forests, and deforestation threatens species including the orangutan, Sumatran tiger, and many species of birds. Removing trees deprives the forest of portions of its canopy, which blocks the sun rays during the day, and retains heat at night. That disruption leads to more extreme temperature swings that can be harmful to plants and animals.

Yet the effects of deforestation reach much farther. The South American rainforest, for example, influences regional and perhaps even global water cycles, and the key to the water supply in Brazilian cities and neighboring countries. The Amazon actually helps furnish water to some of the soy farmers and beef ranchers who are clearing the forest. The loss of clean water and biodiversity from all forests could have many other effects we can't foresee, touching even your morning cup of coffee.

In terms of climate change, cutting trees both adds carbon dioxide to the air and removes the ability to absorb existing carbon dioxide. If tropical deforestation were a country, according to the World Resources Institute, it would rank third in carbon dioxide-equivalent emissions, behind China and the U.S.

Forests and trees make vital contributions to both people and the planet, bolstering livelihoods, providing clean air and water, conserving biodiversity and responding to climate change. Forests act as a source of food, medicine and fuel for more than a billion people. In addition to helping respond to climate change and protect soils and water, forests hold more than three- quarters of the world's terrestrial biodiversity, provide many products and services that contribute to socio- economic development, and are particularly important for hundreds of millions of people in rural areas, including many of the world's poorest.

However, the world's population is projected to increase from around 7.6 billion today to close to 10 billion people by 2050. The corresponding global demand for food estimated to grow by 50 percent during this period is placing enormous pressure on the way we use productive land, particularly in developing countries where the overwhelming majority of the world's 800 million and more poor and hungry people are concentrated. Deforestation, chiefly caused by the conversion of forest land to agriculture and livestock areas, threatens not only the livelihoods of foresters, forest communities and indigenous peoples, but also the variety of life on our planet. Land-use changes result in a loss of valuable habitats, land degradation, soil erosion, a decrease in clean water, and the release of carbon into the atmosphere. How to increase agricultural production and improve food security without reducing forest area is one of the greatest challenges of our times.

ITALY AND NEPAL

Italy - Region of Tuscany

Italy is a high-income country with a population of 61 million, of whom 3.75 million live in Tuscany. Population growth in Italy was 0.23 percent in 2016, and 39 percent of the population lives in rural areas. Forests cover 31.6 percent of Italy's land area and 51 percent of Tuscany, and both shares are increasing. Within Italy, tourism accounts for 13 percent of GDP and agriculture and forestry (combined) for 2.2 percent. Although forest production does not make a significant contribution to the economy, forests and trees are important for broader landscape and watershed management. Following earlier deforestation, the forest area has doubled since 1920 as agriculture has become more intensive and the population more urbanized. Poverty has increased with the economic stagnation of recent years, with 7.6 percent of the population living below the national poverty line.

Tuscany has been a leader in integrated landscape management and was the first region to prepare a Regional Landscape Plan.

Tuscany's forests and trees are valued, for their cultural and ecological value, as well as for their role in traditional rural landscapes, which are important for tourism. The trees are mostly broadleaved, were traditionally coppiced and can serve as important links within ecological networks. They also provide regional food products such as sweet chestnuts, walnuts, hazelnuts and olives. Other benefits include shade for grazing animals and protection for agricultural fields.

Landscape planning integrates economic, social and environmental objectives including rural development, food production, watershed protection, biodiversity and the cultural values of forests and trees within a broad framework of territorial planning. A focus on traditional agriculture and rural landscapes has benefited the economy through tourism and quality food production. Tuscany's approach could have a broader application in countries where landscapes resemble complex mosaics, with tourism, environmental protection and cultural as well as production values. Despite these successes, challenges remain: there are tensions between public policies that focus on regulatory or restrictive approaches and those which support development. There can also be tension between collective and private rights, with different stakeholders having different priorities, and difficulties in balancing tradition and innovation. Furthermore, interdisciplinary approaches to research and science and innovation and conservation can be hard to put into practice.

Nepal

Nepal is a low-income country with a population of 29 million, over 80 percent of whom live in rural areas. Its population is growing at 1.2 percent per year. Forest cover was estimated at 33 percent in 1990 and is now 25.4 percent, although it has stabilized over the last ten years. Forest landscapes vary widely, from mountain to semi- tropical lowland forests and woodlands. Travel and tourism account for 8 percent of GDP and agriculture and forestry for over 30 percent. Poverty rates fell from 38 percent in 2000 to 21.6 percent in 2015, and GDP growth averaged 4.5 percent over the last decade, helped by changing economic structures and remittances. In 2015 Nepal was hit by a devastating earthquake and in 2017 by severe floods. Fuelwood accounts for 85 percent of household energy and for the vast majority of harvested wood. Forests and trees also play a key role in watershed protection and climate resilience and are important for biodiversity and agricultural landscape management. Nepal remains vulnerable to devastating floods and landslides that are caused in part by long-term landscape degradation.

SOLUTIONS:

Plant a tree

In view of increasing urbanization, trees, parks and forests are a must for planners designing the sustainable cities of the future and peri-urban landscapes. Removing pollution, offering shade and contributing to numerous health benefits, greenery is crucial for the well-being of city people, who globally outnumber those living in rural locations. Trees and green spaces in urban areas are also associated with reductions in both childhood obesity and crime, underscoring the links between forests and trees to multiple targets across the 2030 Agenda.

Consume less

The easiest way to cut back on greenhouse gas emissions is simply to buy less stuff. Whether by forgoing an automobile or employing a reusable grocery sack, cutting back on consumption results in fewer fossil fuels being burned to extract, produce and ship products around the globe.

Think green when making purchases. For instance, when in the market for a new car, buy one that will last the longest and have the least impact on the environment. Thus, a used vehicle with a hybrid engine offers superior fuel efficiency over the long haul while saving the environmental impact of new car manufacture.

Paradoxically, when purchasing essentials, such as groceries, buying in bulk can reduce the amount of packaging—plastic wrapping, cardboard boxes and other unnecessary materials. Sometimes buying more means consuming less.

Could I make a difference by changing my diet?

That's a big one, too. In fact, after fossil fuels, the food industry and in particular the meat and dairy sector is one of the most important contributors to climate change.

The meat industry contributes to global warming in many ways. Firstly, cows' burping from processing food releases lots of methane, a greenhouse gas. Secondly, the cows are given antibiotics, to make cows grow at an unnaturally fast rate, the cattle industry implants them with pellets full of hormones. While low levels of naturally occurring hormones are found in various foods, many scientists are concerned that the artificial hormones injected into cows cause health problems in humans who eat them. Many of these hormones are illegal in many countries. Not so delicious, right?

Cows endure routine mutilations, including branding, castration, and dehorning, that cause excruciating, prolonged pain all without painkillers! After months on a severely crowded feedlot, they are then shipped without food or water to a slaughterhouse, where a metal rod is shot through their brains, they are hung upside down, and their throats are slit. Because line speeds are so fast, many animals are still conscious throughout the process.

By reducing your consumption of animal protein by half, you can cut your diet's carbon footprint by more than 40%.

One doesn't have to go vegetarian or vegan to make a difference: cut down gradually and become a 'flexitarian'. By reducing your consumption of animal protein by half, you can cut your diet's carbon footprint by more than 40%.

I CAN'T SEE BUT I CAN FEEL!

Lourdes – Monday 7:00 A.M. 2013

Eyes and heart roll on and pound before me,

where are they going?

They run and stop right in front of Notre Dame's gate.

Stop them!

My soul, was yearning and soliciting from a decade to come here…

Right in the moment when I crossed the iron curtain between
natural and supernatural I understood…

I was swallowed in a blender of bliss and beatitude.

The fragile sisters, all perfectly dressed in blue and white with their celestial heavenly grace, looked like small little helpers of the Blessed Mother...

The kids, wearing on a happy face and smiling were singing next to the river bank, meanwhile the ducks were swimming peacefully. That was one of the places on earth where they weren't afraid of being "mistreated" by men.

Infinite, endless rows of thousands of "sick people" all together, waiting with the young volunteers, chatting happily holding hands, admiring that fabulous place. Full of dignity and pureness they couldn't wait to encounter the Lady dressed in white and blue.

People from all over the world come and pray in this magic place; in this land you perceive something and feel the manifestation.

Then she appears next to me, a blind girl with two shimmering green eyes...

She was smiling because her volunteer friend wanted to take a picture with her!

Who would have ever thought that in Lourdes, a place so far away from her country, she would have felt like being home?

Cuddled but most of all treated like a normal human being.

Today, she didn't feel ashamed for her disability; that annoying sense of piety that common people reserved for her handicap 24/7 was finally fading and drying out.

Tears were running through her face.

This very first time they expressed joy, pure glee.

Mother Mary had just created the miracle. What she had always desired all of a sudden became true: Finally, she was being treated as all the others!

Annie raised her eyes up to the sky, thanking the Almighty in a low voice and said:

"God bless you Notre Dame, they were gifted with sight since birth, but they are so busy looking for your presence, that they can't see you. I'm luckier, I can feel you right here next to me!"

Lourdes – Monday 9:00 P.M. 2013

I gaze at my skin, this very morning I didn't have these scars, my eyes have seen thousands if sick people ready to adore Notre Dame, their purity and dignity paralyzed my soul… They all looked like babies!

I admired her this morning and left this place full of sadness being whirled again in the actual contemporary aquarium.

We decide to stop in Biarritz, to go and eat in a fancy restaurant.

I stare at them.

Oh come on!

Look at these ones!

Parvenus, nouveau riche, all bejeweled, all dressed-up with fur coats and the big golden watches on their wrists capture my attention.

I stare at them, sad faces, all soaked up in a churchy silence, angry in a cold winter day...

My mind involuntarily thinks and noiselessly shouts out loud: "You are the sick and ill ones!"

ANIMAL'S PAS DE CHAT

(Each slaughterhouse should have glass walls)

On today's factory farms, animals are crammed by the thousands into filthy, windowless sheds and stuffed into wire cages, metal crates, and other torturous devices. These animals will never raise their families, root around in the soil, build nests, or do anything that is natural and important to them. Most won't even feel the warmth of the sun on their backs or breathe fresh air until the day they're loaded onto trucks headed for slaughterhouses.

The factory farming industry strives to maximize output while minimizing costs—always at the animals' expense. The giant corporations that run most factory farms have found that they can make more money by squeezing as many animals as possible into tiny spaces, even though many of the animals die from disease or infection.

Animals on factory farms endure constant fear and torment:

They're often given so little space that they can't even turn around or lie down comfortably. Egg-laying hens are kept in small cages, chickens and pigs are kept in jam-packed sheds, and cows are kept on crowded, filthy feedlots.

Antibiotics are used to make animals grow faster and keep them alive in the unsanitary conditions. Scholars show that factory farms' widespread use of antibiotics can lead to antibiotic-resistant bacteria that threaten human health.

Most factory-farmed animals have been genetically manipulated to grow larger and produce more milk or eggs than they naturally would. Some chickens grow so unnaturally large that their legs cannot support their outsized bodies, and they suffer from starvation or dehydration when they can't walk to reach food and water.

When they've grown large enough to slaughter or their bodies have been worn out from producing milk or eggs, animals raised for food are crowded onto trucks and transported for miles through all weather extremes, typically without food or water. At the slaughterhouse, those who survived the transport will have their throats slit, often while they're still conscious. Many remain conscious when they're plunged into the scalding-hot water of the de-feathering or hair-removal tanks or while their bodies are being skinned or hacked apart.

Elephants, tigers, and other animals that circuses use to entertain audiences do not stand on their heads, jump through hoops, or balance on pedestals because they want to. They perform these and other difficult tricks because they're afraid of what will happen if they don't.

To force animals to perform, circus trainers abuse them with whips, tight collars, muzzles, electric prods, bull hooks (heavy batons with a sharp steel hook on one end), and other painful tools of the circus trade. Video footage of animal training sessions shows that elephants are beaten with bull hooks and shocked with electric prods. Circuses easily get away with such routine cruelty because the government doesn't monitor training sessions and handlers are cautious when they're in public.

Circuses travel nearly year-round in all weather extremes, sometimes for days at a time. While in transit, the animals are confined to trailers or trucks, where they may not have access to basic necessities, such as food, water, and veterinary care. Elephants are chained, and big cats are imprisoned in cramped, filthy cages, in which they eat, drink, sleep, defecate, and urinate— all in the same place. And there's no relief once the animals reach a venue, where they remain caged and are chained in arena basements and parking lots.

So Please,

Tell me,

How would you feel?

AN ARABESQUE ON THE WORLD

(On Traveling)

Cold winter day, it's raining non-stop here in the UK, I find myself in Chester, a beautiful city mounted in the region of Wales, for a couple of weeks...

Sitting on a Starbuck's sofa I am looking out of the window, breathe in, new smells, different people, places to discover, things to learn.

This could be the intro of my topic this morning, voilà, trenchant.

Definitely what's going on in my life at 9:43 A.M.

Last week, shrink told us, that nowadays a lot of tragedies occur because people are always running around, he said that we don't look at each other in the eyes anymore, we don't pay attention if someone is in need or not.

Many youngsters unfortunately, get to the point of no return, they commit suicide. Let me tell you, this phenomenon is increasing perilously.

No co-mmunication, no results.

We think we are all so connected to each other thanks to social media and to the internet that we have become the oxymoron of ourselves.

Is this social world really positive for our mental health?

But then I scroll out of this Welsh window, sipping my coffee, ferociously I stare at them, people holding their hands, laughing, it's the time of the year when we celebrate Christmas, here the fairy lights are simply amazing, bright and colored, it was a long of time I didn't sense this magic in the air.

While I'm writing these words, black and white during this grey day on my Mac,

a man with his wife enters the café.

She is on a wheelchair and he helps her in every possible way, if I raise my head I can see her right in front of me, she's got blue sparkling eyes and her legs are covered by a funny elephant blanket.

He goes to get her a lemon muffin and she tells me smiling:

"I'm excited he doesn't take me out very often!"

But they are so sweet, he serves her the frappuccino and tells her:

"Here you are my darling."

Not only I realize she's on a wheelchair but she can't move at all, her arms and legs are paralyzed.

Can't stop looking at them, how does it feel to be totally petrified?

This little story, that's happening right now, in this very moment is the answer to everything.

Especially to all of the kids and friends that have taken their lives away, there are people out there struggling to survive, to stand on two legs, to overcome a bad illness or a trauma.

Maybe, you shouldn't follow your gut but think before acting and throwing your life away.

This woman in front of me is literally paralyzed but she's fighting alone in order to stay alive!

If we look at our life from another perspective, we'll understand loads of things hidden before.

Life is what you make of it, you are the choices you take every single instant, we have to live each day as it were our last. This is the reason why I have decided to travel and to live fully.

One of the traditions in our family is, after a trip, to open our suitcases and take out all of the gifts and stuff bought from our journeys, I'll never forget my mom and dad creating magic out of this process every time we came back home.

Nowadays many people travel and live, to post, just to show their "social friends" that they have been somewhere. It has become a colossal business, namely Instagram and Facebook have ruined travel too, everything seems jumbled up and the prices of the tickets have skyrocketed due to this issue.

Apart from this, there are plenty of things one can gain from exploring different places. The list includes gaining new friends, new experiences, and new stories.

When you start exploring new places, you get a better understanding of the people living there, including their culture, traditions, history and background.

Studies show that travelling can improve your overall health and enhance your creativity. Therefore, you need to take time out from your daily tasks, office responsibilities, hectic schedule, and everyday pressures at least once in a year. Plan a tour to a new city with an open schedule and let life present you with the numerous opportunities.

One of the main benefits of travelling, especially to areas where your native language is not widely used, is that you learn how to communicate better with other people. Brushing up your knowledge on the most commonly used phrases or questions tourists ask can help you reach out to and relate better with the locals.

We all have stress and tension in our lives. Travelling forces us to temporarily disconnect from our normal routine, helping us appreciate the people and things we have around. As per a famous saying "we never know what we have until we lose it."

It is believed that if someone gets out of their comfort zone, the mind gets more creative.

To develop new neural connections that trigger original and creative thoughts, you must explore new places and break out of your daily routine.

 I always get a strange and sad feeling when I get back from places like India for example.

When I happen to meet someone that has a different lifestyle and mindset I reject sharing my ideas, the world is full of boring people that refuse to get out of their comfort zones, they become ignorant, close minded and start thinking mainly about superficial and useless things.

As Pablo Neruda's Ode to life says:

Dies slowly…

He who becomes the slave of habit,
who follows the same routes every day,
who never changes pace,
who does not risk and change the color of his clothes,
who does not speak and does not experience,
dies slowly.

He or she who shuns passion,
who prefers black on white,
dotting ones „it's" rather than a bundle of emotions, the kind that
make your eyes glimmer,
that turn a yawn into a smile,
that make the heart pound in the face of mistakes and feelings,
dies slowly.

He or she who does not turn things topsy-turvy,
who is unhappy at work,
who does not risk certainty for uncertainty,
to thus follow a dream,
those who do not forego sound advice at least once in their lives,
die slowly.

He who does not travel, who does not read,
who does not listen to music,
who does not find grace in himself,
she who does not find grace in herself,
dies slowly.

He who slowly destroys his own self-esteem,
who does not allow himself to be helped,
who spends days on end complaining about his own bad luck, about
the rain that never stops,
dies slowly.

He or she who abandon a project before starting it, who fail to ask
questions on subjects he doesn't know, he or she who don't reply when
they are asked something they do know,
die slowly.

Let's try and avoid death in small doses,
reminding oneself that being alive requires an effort far greater than the
simple fact of breathing.

Only a burning patience will lead
to the attainment of a splendid happiness.

While travelling, you will find yourself stuck in situations where things don't always go as planned. Such situations will help you learn to tackle the uncertainties in life.

Being in a place where you do not know anyone will assist you to gain confidence and presence of mind. You will develop the ability to cope with obstacles, which will make you a confident person.

Meeting different people from vast cultures and societies provides an education that is impossible to get in a traditional school, college or a university. There is no substitute for the real thing.

If you travel with friends and family members, travelling helps you build stronger bonds and make memories.

When you travel, you do not care what you do at all and you can just break free from the norm.

While travelling, you might find yourself stuck in situations you won't normally experience in your daily life. This can help you understand yourself and how you react to such circumstances, preparing you for future similar situations.

Remember, you only live once, so start travelling and get some life-altering experiences.

THE LONG AND WINDING JOURNEY

The trees with their

big

black

dry

branches

seem as though they'd want to frame the Almighty creatures.

Cubs that grow

with

then

out of the blue

without

their mamas.

Drained animals that witness a different scenario:

Elephants

Lions

Zebras

Rhinos

Giraffes

Hyenas

walking in the same direction for

hundred

thousands

of kilometers

all together.

Thirsty

hungry

tired.

Marching for what?

How do you feel when you are starving?

You don't want to know…

Facing all the worse climates

only to reach that lake

walking for days

and on those tracks many have died…

Some for those vicious poachers,

they told me that they land

with their helicopters on the desert's dry land

kill the rhinos

steal their horns

and leave them there…

They showed to my eyes things that humans should not even
dream about doing.

I saw those lakes where they all gather.

Africa's not the one that you see on google images,

her animals have disappeared

they all lay dead on the river bank

because when they get there they find nothing to drink and they die.

No rain

No water

No life…

But the sun will go down also tonight and become a huge

bright

flaming

red ball

now, just for a few seconds

he's the main character.

Magnificently red.

Red like this ground that resembles the color of the blood reflecting on the sun, once he decides to go sleep with Simba and his family, hoping that tomorrow won't be the last day of their life.

Animals have learnt how to pray.

They pray

hoping that

humans

will

understand and STOP!

Yes, you'll never see a sunset greater than the one in Africa.

Bibliography

Consulted websites
http://www.fao.org/home/en/
https://www.greenpeace.it
https://www.un.org
https://www.nytimes.com/
https://www.bbc.com/news/world
https://www.thechignontraveler.com

}